Claude
DEBUSSY
PETITE SUITE
CD 71B
Orchestrated by
Henri Büsser
Edited by
Richard W. Sargeant, Jr.

Study Score
Partitur

SERENISSIMA MUSIC, INC.

ORCHESTRA

2 Flutes (2nd also Piccolo)

2 Oboes (2nd also English Horn)

2 Clarinets (B-flat)

2 Bassoons

4 Horns (F)

2 Trumpets (C)

Timpani
Cymbals, Triangle, Tambourine

Harp

Violin I

Violin II

Viola

Violoncello

Double Bass

Duration: ca. 13 minutes

Premiere: November 4, 1907
Paris, Concerts Lamoureaux
Orchestre Lamoureaux / Camille Chevillard

ISMN: 979-0-58042-118-0
This score is a newly engraved urtext edition primarily
based upon the first edition of the full score and part
issued in Paris by Durand et Fils in 1907.

Printed in the USA
First Printing: August, 2018

PETITE SUITE
CD 71b
1. En Bateau

Claude Debussy
Orchestrated by Henri Büsser
Edited by Richard W. Sargeant, Jr.

42301

4

11
Fl. 1 2
mf
p sost.
Ob. 1 2
1.
pp
legg.
Cl. 1 2
pp
legg.
Bn. 1 2
Hn. 1 2
1.
poco
Tpt. 1 2
Timp.
pp
Tgl. Cymb.
pp
Hp.
p
pp
11
Vn. 1
unis.
sul g
poco
pp
p espress.
poco
2
poco
pp
Va.
dim.
pp
Vc.
unis.
dim.
pp
dim.
ppp
Cb.
arco
dim.
ppp

17
16
Fl. 1 2
a2
Ob. 1 2
Cl. 1 2
a2
Bn. 1 2
Hn. 1 2
Tpt. 1 2
Timp.
Tgl. Cymb.
Hp.
cresc.
Vn. 1 2
ord.
Va.
pp espress.
poco
cresc.
div.
Vc.
pizz.
Cb.

21
Fl. 1 2
mf
dim.
p
pp
Ob. 1 2
1.
p
pp
Cl. 1 2
1.
mf
dim.
p
pp
Bn. 1 2
Hn. 1 2
pp
Tpt. 1 2
Timp.
Tgl. Cymb.
Hp.
mf
p
pp
21
Vn. 1
mf
p
div.
pp
Vn. 2
mf
div. pizz.
pp
Va.
div.
unis.
mf
pp
ppp
Vc.
div.
pizz.
mf
p
pp
Cb.
mf

8

42301

33
Fl. 1 2
Ob. 1 2
a2
Cl. 1 2
Bn. 1 2
Hn. 1 2
f molto ritmo
Tpt. 1 2
Timp.
Tgl. Cymb.
Hp.
sons étouffes
Vn. 1 2
più f
Va.
più f molto ritmo
Vc.
Cb.

40
45
Fl. 1 2
Ob. 1 2
Cl. 1 2
Bn. 1 2
Hn. 1 2
Tpt. 1 2
Timp.
Tgl. Cymb.
Hp.
Vn. 1 2
Va.
Vc.
Cb.
a2
1.
p
mf
dim.
f
pp
sus. cymb.
(with timp. sticks)
pizz.
arco
div.
unis.

46
Fl. 1 2
Ob. 1 2
Cl. 1 2
Bn. 1 2
Hn. 1 2
Tpt. 1 2
Timp.
Tgl. Cymb.
Hp.
Vn. 1 2
Va.
Vc.
Cb.
1.
a2
p legg.
mf
p poco
pp
div.
pizz.
1 desk
tutti

12

42301

59
Fl. 1 2
Ob. 1 2
Cl. 1 2
Bn. 1 2
Hn. 1 2
Tpt. 1 2
Timp.
Tgl. Cymb.
Hp.
Vn. 1 2
Va.
Vc.
Cb.
a2
1.
con sord.
f
mf
p
pp
dim.
mf en dehors
p dolce espress.
f très en dehors
pizz.
arco
arco div.

Un peu retenu

75
a tempo
73
a2
Fl. 1 2
Ob. 1 2
Cl. 1 2
Bn. 1 2
Hn. 1 2
Tpt. 1 2
Timp.
Tgl. Cymb.
Hp.
p
poco
pp
dim.
ppp
mf
Vn. 1 2
Va.
Vc.
Cb.
dolce espress.
div.

78
Fl. 1 2
poco
Ob. 1 2
Cl. 1 2
Bn. 1 2
Hn. 1 2
p
Tpt. 1 2
1.
p
Timp.
Tgl. Cymb.
Hp.
78
Vn. 1
2
Va.
Vc.
Cb.

85
82
Fl. 1 2
p
p
Ob. 1 2
1.
p un peu en
Cl. 1 2
poco
pp
Bn. 1 2
poco
pp
Hn. 1 2
poco
p
Tpt. 1 2
poco
p
Timp.
Tgl. Cymb.
Hp.
p
cresc.
mf
82
85
Vn. 1
sost.
p
Vn. 2
pizz.
p
arco
Va.
poco
p
poco
p
Vc.
unis.
poco
p
Cb.
p

86
Fl. 1 2
Ob. 1 2
Cl. 1 2
Bn. 1 2
Hn. 1 2
Tpt. 1 2
Timp.
Tgl. Cymb.
Hp.
Vn. 1 2
Va.
Vc.
Cb.
dehors
pp
p legg.
p
p dim.
pp
a2
mf
dim.
arco
legg.

91
93
Fl. 1 2
pp
Ob. 1 2
p
Cl. 1 2
1.
p espress.
a2
Bn. 1 2
Hn. 1 2
pp
dim.
Tpt. 1 2
Timp.
Tgl. Cymb.
Hp.
Vn. 1 2
molto
unis.
Va.
ppp
Vc.
1 desk
pizz.
Cb.

97
En retenant peu à peu
Fl. 1 2
Ob. 1 2
Cl. 1 2
più p
dim.
Bn. 1 2
Hn. 1 2
ppp
Tpt. 1 2
Timp.
Tgl.
Cymb.
Hp.
pp
p
97
En retenant peu à peu
Vn.
1
2
dim.
ppp
ppp
Va.
div.
Vc.
tutti
div.
Cb.
pp

Encore plus retenu

2. Cortege

Moderato
Flute 1 2
Oboe 1 2
Clarinet (B♭) 1 2
Bassoon 1 2
Horn (F) 1 2
C Trumpet 1 2
Timpani
Triangle Cymbals
Harp
Moderato
Violin 1 2
Viola
Violoncello
Contrabass
pizz.
a2
poco
p
pp

42301

7
Fl. 1 2
a2
mf
Ob. 1 2
1.
p
dim.
pp
cresc.
Cl. 1 2
a2
mf
Bn. 1 2
p
dim.
pp
Hn. 1 2
1.
p
dim.
pp
Tpt. 1 2
Timp.
Tgl. Cymb.
p
Hp.
mf
dim.
p
7
Vn.
1
arco
pp
p
cresc.
2
arco
pp
p
cresc.
Va.
pp
p
cresc.
Vc.
div.
pp
p
cresc.
Cb.
pizz.
pp
p
cresc.

11
10
Fl. 1 2
Ob. 1 2
Cl. 1 2
Bn. 1 2
Hn. 1 2
Tpt. 1 2
Timp.
Tgl. Cymb.
Hp.
p subito
p
a2
sus. cymb.
(with timp. sticks)
11
10
Vn. 1 2
Va.
Vc.
Cb.
pizz.
unis.
arco

Brillant

poco rit.

22 a tempo scherzando
Fl. 1 2
Ob. 1 2
Cl. 1 2
Bn. 1 2
1.
p mf
Hn. 1 2
mf p
Tpt. 1 2
Timp.
Tgl. Cymb.
Hp.
mf
22 a tempo scherzando
Vn. 1 2
Va.
Vc.
Cb.
p
arco
pizz.
div. arco
mf

26
Fl. 1 2
mf
Ob. 1 2
1.
p
Cl. 1 2
p
Bn. 1 2
Hn. 1 2
mp
p
Tpt. 1 2
Timp.
p
Tgl. Cymb.
Hp.
p
26
Vn. 1 2
p
Va.
p
unis.
Vc.
p
pizz.
Cb.

29
Fl. 1 2
dim.
p
a2
Ob. 1 2
pp
Cl. 1 2
1.
mp
p
pp
a2
Bn. 1 2
pp
Hn. 1 2
pp
Tpt. 1 2
poco mf
p
Timp.
pp
Tgl. Cymb.
pp
sus. cymb.
(with timp. sticks)
p
Hp.
pp
mf
29
Vn. 1 2
pizz.
dim.
pp
p
arco
Va.
pizz.
arco
dim.
pp
p
Vc.
pizz.
arco
pp
p
Cb.
pp
p

34
32
Fl. 1 2
a2
cresc. poco a poco
Ob. 1 2
Cl. 1 2
cresc. poco a poco
Bn. 1 2
1.
Hn. 1 2
Tpt. 1 2
poco mf
Timp.
Tgl. Cymb.
Hp.
mf
34
32
Vn. 1
arco
cresc. poco a poco
2
pizz.
Va.
pizz.
arco
pizz.
Vc.
pizz.
arco
pizz.
Cb.
div.
unis.

35
Fl. 1 2
p
p
Ob. 1 2
p
Cl. 1 2
p
p
Bn. 1 2
p
Hn. 1 2
Tpt. 1 2
Timp.
Tgl. Cymb.
p
Hp.
p
sons étouffes
sons étouffes
35
tr
tr
Vn. 1
p espress.
dim.
2
arco
mf
p
dim.
Va.
arco
mf
p espress. en dehors
dim.
Vc.
arco
mf
p espress. en dehors
dim.
Cb.
mf
p
pp

34

42301

43 **Tempo I**

44
Fl. 1 2
Ob. 1 2
p
poco
Cl. 1 2
Bn. 1 2
Hn. 1 2
Tpt. 1 2
p
Timp.
Tgl. Cymb.
Hp.
44
Vn. 1
p
pp
unis.
2
p
pp
Va.
p
pp
arco
Vc.
arco
Cb.

47
Fl. 1 2
pp
Ob. 1 2
pp
1.
pp
Cl. 1 2
pp
Bn. 1 2
pp
Hn. 1 2
1.
pp
senza sord.
Tpt. 1 2
Timp.
Tgl. Cymb.
pp
Hp.
p
47
Vn. 1
pp
2
pp
Va.
pp
pp
Vc.
pp
pp
Cb.
p
dim.
pp

53
50
Fl. 1 2
a2
mf
Ob. 1 2
cresc.
Cl. 1 2
Bn. 1 2
Hn. 1 2
Tpt. 1 2
p
Timp.
Tgl. Cymb.
sus. cymb.
(with timp. sticks)
Hp.
f
Vn. 1 2
pizz.
p
cresc.
Va.
div.
unis.
Vc.
Cb.
arco

54
Fl. 1 2
Ob. 1 2
Cl. 1 2
Bn. 1 2
Hn. 1 2
Tpt. 1 2
Timp.
Tgl. Cymb.
Hp.
Vn. 1
2
Va.
Vc.
Cb.
a2
arco
dim.
cresc.
p
mf
f

Brillant

Brillant

riten.
59
a2
Fl. 1 2
ff
Ob. 1 2
ff
Cl. 1 2
ff
Bn. 1 2
ff
Hn. 1 2
a2
Tpt. 1 2
a2
più f
ff
Timp.
Tgl. Cymb.
f
ff
Hp.
riten.
59
Vn. 1
ff
2
ff
Va.
ff
Vc.
Cb.

61
Fl. 1 2
Ob. 1 2
2. to E. H.
Cl. 1 2
Bn. 1 2
Hn. 1 2
Tpt. 1 2
Timp.
ff
Tgl.
Cymb.
ff
Hp.
fff
m.d.
61
Vn.
1
2
non div.
Va.
non div.
Vc.
non div.
ff
Cb.
ff

3. Menuet

44

14
17
Fl. 1 2
Ob.
E. H.
Cl. 1 2
Bn. 1 2
Hn. 1 2
Hp.
f
p
14
17
Vn.
1
2
Va.
Vc.
Cb.
mf
dim.
p
f
mf

19
1.
Fl. 1 2
p
p
Ob.
p
poco
E. H.
p
poco
1.
Cl. 1 2
pp
p
Bn. 1 2
pp
poco cresc.
Hn. 1 2
Hp.
19
Vn.
1
pp
p
2
pp
p
arco
Va.
pp
p
Vc.
p
mf
Cb.

23
Fl. 1 2
Ob.
p dim. pp
E. H.
p dim. pp
p
Cl. 1 2
Bn. 1 2
p dim. pp
Hn. 1 2
pp poco cresc.
Hp.
p
23
Vn. 1
p pp
div.
Vn. 2
p pp p
div.
Va.
dim. pp
p espress.
poco cresc.
p
Vc.
p
div.
arco
Cb.
p pp p

32
29
Fl. 1 2
Ob.
p
f
E. H.
Cl. 1 2
Bn. 1 2
1.
p grazioso
Hn. 1 2
Hp.
Vn.
unis.
senza sord.
poco cresc.
pizz.
arco
Va.
pp
Vc.
unis.
pizz.
Cb.
mf

35
Fl. 1 2
Ob.
E. H.
Cl. 1 2
Bn. 1 2
Hn. 1 2
Hp.
Vn. 1 2
Va.
Vc.
Cb.
pp
p grazioso
p
a2
poco
pp

41
Fl. 1 2
pp
Ob.
pp
mf senza pesante
E. H.
pp
Cl. 1 2
pp
Bn. 1 2
pp
mf senza pesante
Hn. 1 2
Hp.
41
Vn. 1
mf p
mf
dim
2
mf
mf
Va.
tr
mf
mf
p
Vc.
mf
pp
mf
pp
Cb.
arco
pizz.
arco
pizz.
mf
p
mf
p

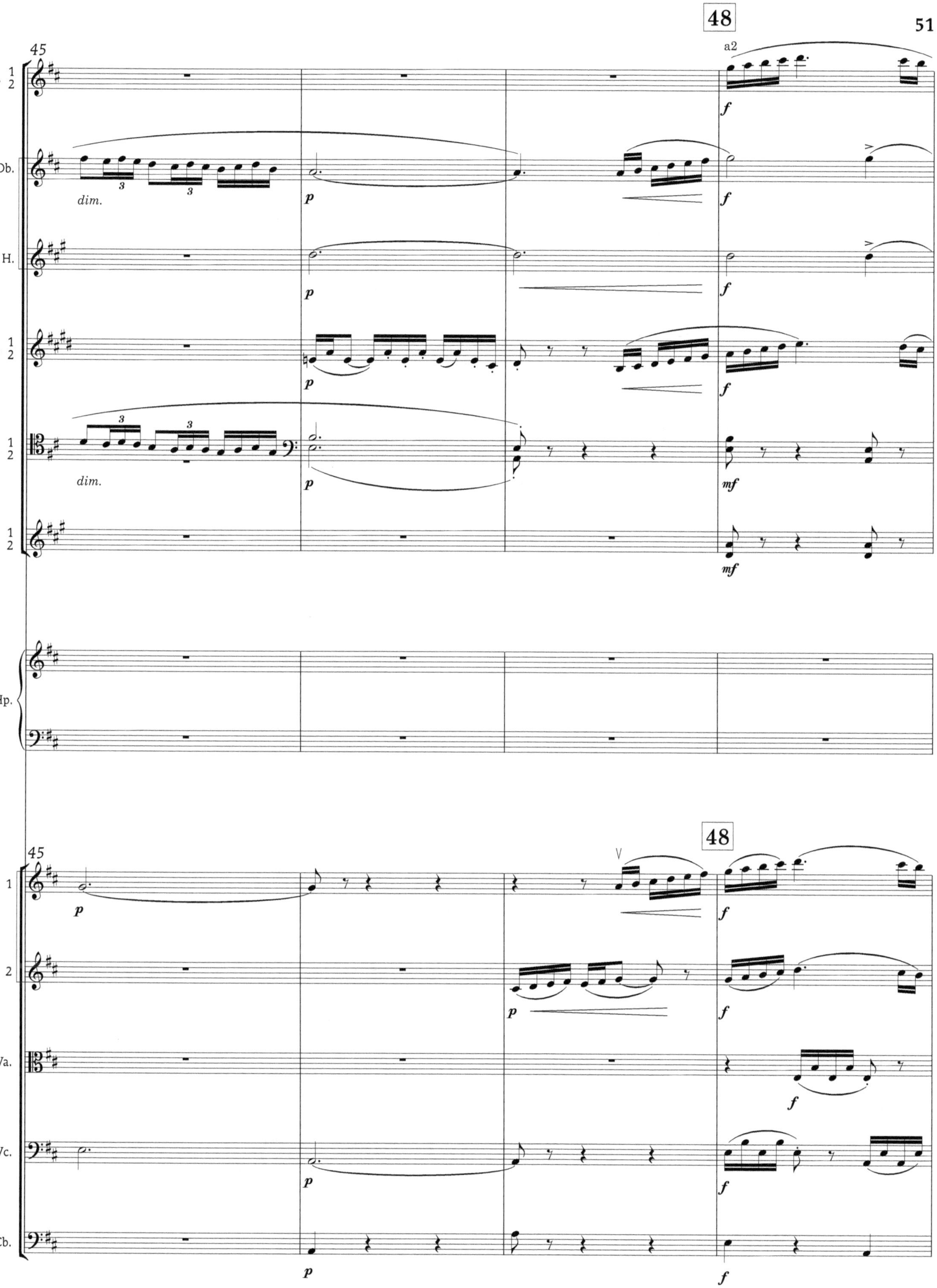
48
45
a2
Fl. 1 2
Ob.
dim.
E. H.
Cl. 1 2
Bn. 1 2
dim.
Hn. 1 2
Hp.
45
48
Vn. 1
2
Va.
Vc.
Cb.

49
Fl. 1 2
Ob.
E. H.
Cl. 1 2
Bn. 1 2
a2
Hn. 1 2
Hp.
49
Vn.
1
2
div.
div.
Va.
pizz
Vc.
pizz
Cb.

54
Fl. 1 2
Ob.
E. H.
Cl. 1 2
Bn. 1 2
Hn. 1 2
Hp.
Vn. 1 2
Va.
Vc.
Cb.
p
più p
pp
ppp
a2
p un peu en dehors
1.
dim.

59
60
Fl. 1 2
1.
p
Ob.
p espress.
E. H.
p
dim.
Cl. 1 2
1.
p
dim.
Bn. 1 2
Hn. 1 2
Hp.
p
59
60
Vn.
1
con sord.
2
con sord.
Va.
arco
pp
Vc.
div.
arco
pp
unis.
Cb.
p

63
Fl. 1 2
Ob.
E. H.
Cl. 1 2
Bn. 1 2
Hn. 1 2
Hp.
Vn. 1 2
Va.
Vc.
Cb.
pp (echo)
p dolce espress.
unis.
sempre pp
poco

68
Fl. 1 2
Ob.
E. H.
Cl. 1 2
Bn. 1 2
Hn. 1 2
1.
p
pp
poco
1. con sord.
Hp.
Vn. 1
2
Va.
Vc.
Cb.

73
76
Fl. 1 2
Ob.
E. H.
Cl. 1 2
Bn. 1 2
Hn. 1 2
Hp.
Vn. 1 2
Va.
Vc.
Cb.
p
dim.
pp
p dolce espress.
1.
poco
1. (con sord.)
pizz.

78
Fl. 1 2
Ob.
E. H.
Cl. 1 2
Bn. 1 2
Hn. 1 2
Hp.
Vn. 1 2
Va.
Vc.
Cb.
p
pp
dim.
1.
senza sord.
sons étouffes

83
Fl. 1 2
ppp
pp
2. to pic.
Ob.
ppp
E. H.
to ob.
Cl. 1 2
pp (echo)
ppp
1.
Bn. 1 2
pp (echo)
Hn. 1 2
Hp.
pp
83
senza sord.
Vn. 1
ppp
senza sord.
2
ppp
arco
Va.
pp
pizz.
pp
arco
Vc.
pp
pizz.
pp
Cb.
pp

4. Ballet

Allegro giusto
Piccolo
Flute
Oboe 1 2
Clarinet (B♭) 1 2
Bassoon 1 2
Horn (F) 1 2
C Trumpet 1 2
Timpani
Triangle
Cymbals
Tambourine
Harp
Allegro giusto
sul g
sul d
Violin 1 2
Viola
Violoncello
Contrabass

10
Picc.
Fl.
Ob. 1 2
Cl. 1 2
Bn. 1 2
Hn. 1 2
Tpt. 1 2
Timp.
Tgl. Cymb.
Tamb.
Hp.
Vn. 1 2
Va.
Vc.
Cb.
a2
cresc.
pizz.
arco

62

42301

21
26
Picc.
Fl.
Ob. 1 2
Cl. 1 2
Bn. 1 2
Hn. 1 2
Tpt. 1 2
Timp.
Tgl. Cymb.
Tamb.
Hp.
Vn. 1 2
Va.
Vc.
Cb.
a2
pizz.
arco
p
pp

27
Picc.
Fl.
Ob. 1 2
Cl. 1 2
Bn. 1 2
a2
Hn. 1 2
Tpt. 1 2
Timp.
Tgl. Cymb.
Tamb.
Hp.
Vn. 1 2
Va.
Vc.
Cb.
cresc. poco a poco
p cresc. poco a poco
arco
pizz.
f

33
Picc.
Fl.
Ob. 1 2
a2
Cl. 1 2
a2
Bn. 1 2
Hn. 1 2
Tpt. 1 2
Timp.
Tgl. Cymb.
Tamb.
Hp.
33
Vn. 1 2
Va.
div.
Vc.
arco
Cb.
arco
pizz.

40
39
Picc.
Fl.
Ob. 1 2
Cl. 1 2
Bn. 1 2
Hn. 1 2
Tpt. 1 2
Timp.
Tgl. Cymb.
Tamb.
Hp.
a2 cuivrez
p (echo)
più f
crash cymb.
40
39
Vn. 1 2
Va.
Vc.
Cb.
unis.
arco
sul ponticello

Tempo di Valse
50 a tempo (♩. = 72)
48 rit.
Picc.
Fl.
Ob. 1 2
Cl. 1 2
Bn. 1 2
Hn. 1 2
Tpt. 1 2
Timp.
Tgl. Cymb.
Tamb.
Hp.
2.
a2
1.
cresc.
poco
Tempo di Valse
50 a tempo (♩. = 72)
48 rit.
Vn. 1
2
Va.
Vc.
Cb.
sul g
sul d
pizz.
cresc.
poco

58
Picc.
Fl.
Ob. 1 2
Cl. 1 2
Bn. 1 2
a2
Hn. 1 2
1.
Tpt. 1 2
Timp.
Tgl. Cymb.
Tamb.
Hp.
58
Vn. 1 2
Va.
Vc.
Cb.

68
Picc.
Fl.
p cresc.
Ob. 1 2
1.
p très espress.
cresc.
Cl. 1 2
1.
cresc.
Bn. 1 2
p
cresc.
Hn. 1 2
1.
p
cresc.
a2
Tpt. 1 2
Timp.
Tgl. Cymb.
Tamb.
Hp.
68
Vn. 1 2
Va.
p
cresc. poco a poco
Vc.
p très espress.
cresc. poco a poco
pizz.
arco
Cb.
cresc.

76
Picc.
Fl.
Ob. 1 2
a2
Cl. 1 2
a2
Bn. 1 2
dim.
Hn. 1 2
dim.
con sord.
Tpt. 1 2
Timp.
Tgl. Cymb.
Tamb.
Hp.
sons étouffes
76
Vn. 1
mf espress.
Vn. 2
mf espress.
en dehors
Va.
dim.
Vc.
mf espress.
Cb.
pizz.

83
86
Picc.
Fl.
Ob. 1 2
Cl. 1 2
Bn. 1 2
Hn. 1 2
Tpt. 1 2
Timp.
Tgl. Cymb.
Tamb.
Hp.
Vn. 1 2
Va.
Vc.
Cb.
dim.
pp
poco
p
ppp
mf
sul g
poco a poco
pizz.
arco

poco rit.
a tempo
92
Picc.
Fl.
Ob. 1 2
Cl. 1 2
Bn. 1 2
Hn. 1 2
Tpt. 1 2
Timp.
Tgl. Cymb.
Tamb.
Hp.
pp
poco
p
a2
con sord.
(con sord.)
sus. cymb. (with timp. stick)
poco rit.
a tempo
92
Vn. 1 2
Va.
Vc.
Cb.
sul g
pizz.
arco
mf
pp
p

107 **Tempo I**

108
Picc.
Fl.
Ob. 1 2
Cl. 1 2
Bn. 1 2
cresc.
f
p
Hn. 1 2
Tpt. 1 2
molto
senza sord.
Timp.
Tgl. Cymb.
Tamb.
cresc. molto
Hp.
mf
6
3
108
Vn. 1 2
Va.
Vc.
Cb.
arco
sul g

113
Picc.
Fl.
Ob. 1 2
Cl. 1 2
Bn. 1 2
Hn. 1 2
Tpt. 1 2
Timp.
Tgl. Cymb.
Tamb.
Hp.
Vn. 1 2
Va.
Vc.
Cb.
a2
mf
p
f
cresc.
sul d
arco
pizz.

119

125
Picc.
Fl.
Ob. 1 2
Cl. 1 2
Bn. 1 2
Hn. 1 2
a2
Tpt. 1 2
Timp.
Tgl. Cymb.
sus. cymb.
(with timp. stick)
Tamb.
Hp.
125
Vn. 1
2
pizz.
arco
sul d
Va.
Vc.
Cb.
p
pp
mf

135
131
Picc.
Fl.
Ob. 1 2
Cl. 1 2
Bn. 1 2
Hn. 1 2
Tpt. 1 2
Timp.
Tgl. Cymb.
Tamb.
Hp.
Vn. 1 2
Va.
Vc.
Cb.
a2
pizz.
arco
p
pp

136
Picc.
Fl.
Ob. 1 2
Cl. 1 2
Bn. 1 2
a2
Hn. 1 2
Tpt. 1 2
Timp.
Tgl.
Cymb.
Tamb.
Hp.
Vn. 1 2
Va.
Vc.
Cb.
arco
cresc. poco a poco
p cresc. poco a poco

143 Mouvt de Valse (a un temps)

143 Mouvt de Valse (a un temps)

149
Picc.
Fl.
Ob. 1 2
p
Cl. 1 2
p
Bn. 1 2
p
Hn. 1 2
p
Tpt. 1 2
Timp.
Tgl. Cymb.
Tamb.
Hp.
mf
149
Vn. 1
mf
p
Vn. 2
mf
p
unis.
Va.
p espress.
Vc.
p espress.
pizz.
Cb.
div.
p
pizz.
p

155
Picc.
Fl.
Ob. 1 2
Cl. 1 2
Bn. 1 2
Hn. 1 2
Tpt. 1 2
Timp.
Tgl. Cymb.
crash cymb.
Tamb.
Hp.
cresc. molto
cresc. poco a poco
155
pizz.
arco
Vn. 1 2
Va.
Vc.
Cb.

Animé
163
Picc.
Fl.
Ob. 1 2
Cl. 1 2
a2
Bn. 1 2
Hn. 1 2
Tpt. 1 2
Timp.
Tgl. Cymb.
Tamb.
Hp.
ff
f
Animé
163
Vn. 1 2
Va.
Vc.
Cb.
unis.
sff
ff